Diary of a Divorce

Diary of a Divorce
S. D. CURTIS

2020

Published by Arc Publications,
Nanholme Mill, Shaw Wood Road
Todmorden OL14 6DA, UK
www.arcpublications.co.uk

Copyright in the poems © S. D. Curtis, 2020
Copyright in the present edition © Arc Publications, 2020

The right of S. D. Curtis to be identified as the author
of this work has been asserted by her in accordance with
the Copyright, Designs and Patents Act 1988.

978 1910345 16 0

Design by Tony Ward
Printed in the UK by ImprintDigital.com,
Upton Pyne, Exeter, Devon

The cover illustration is a detail from
'The Girl from Soho' by Yusuf Elsaadi,
by kind permission of the artist.

This book is in copyright. Subject to statutory exception
and to provision of relevant collective licensing
agreements, no reproduction of any part
of this book may take place without the written
permission of Arc Publications.

Arc Chapbook Series
Series Editor: Tony Ward

CONTENTS

Anniversary Gift / 11
Flight / 13
Bookends / 14
A Little Time / 15
My Story / 16
Dignity / 17
Underwritten / 18
Dead Weight / 19
Unanswered / 20
Writing Poems / 21
Future, Imagined / 23
Divorce / 24
Inheritance / 25
Not Anger / 27
To You / 28
Story / 29
The Last Page / 33

Biographical Note / 35

For my (ex) husband
The Banker

"Yet the promise is not of a monument. (Who, still on a battlefield, wants monuments?) The promise is that language has acknowledged, has given shelter, to the experience which demanded, which cried out."

JOHN BERGER, *And Our Faces, My Heart, Brief as Photos* (2005)

ANNIVERSARY GIFT

Paper, wood, bronze,
so the years are fêted.
I started well,
a circus curiosity,
a girl who speaks
your tongue,
whose tongue
is entwined with yours

I vow to seal
the fairy tale.
I will be the one
who breaks the pattern,
whose love will last,
whose man is fast

Ten years in
and instead of tin,
I spit truth
like blood

By year sixteen,
I am a ghost
Can you see how I shine?
Like parchment,
like sinews stretched

Soon it will be time
for fragile china
But I have no gift to bring
– *pa-rup-a-pum-pum* –
just the sum

of who I am
spelled out on a headboard.
Just the hurt
of who I am
sewn into my jawbone.

Shall we toast
with this concoction
of bodily fluids?
Shall we feast
on a crime?

It is juicy enough,
if a little long
in the tooth
and old hens, they say,
make the best soup.

FLIGHT

My wedding ring took flight
last night. Across the rooftops
across the sky above our heads

By chance a magpie might
be attracted by its glint
oblivious of the inscription
wildly immune to human bonds

Or might its beak stick
fast inside the golden band
rendering it dumb, unable
to communicate 'Help me!'

Or its foot become
bound by the weight of gold
shackled by promises made
by another species

We are dumb animals too
– flightless and graceless –
holding on too long to wedding rings
that long to be set in orbit

BOOKENDS

Did you still love me then?

As they sanded down the corners
of the shelves where we rested our books
As they manoeuvred the piano

around the stairwell – ballet dancers
in overalls moving in tune to a silent symphony
of equilibrium – like lovers
anticipating each shift of body weight

Did you love me then?

As the moon trafficked across
our curtain-less window,
tracing the arc of hours
Our first night in our first house

Or had you already blanched at
the lines in the corners of my eyes,
the loose flesh above the scar
where our child escaped my womb

And with that thought of escape
perhaps a realization
that there was only one door,
a hall too narrow for us to exit together

but only one by one
and someone had to be first:
Our child. Your wife. Or you.

A LITTLE TIME

If you had had a little time
(between calls, texts, emails)
we could have risen above,
invented a surname that was only ours:
free of the sins of our fathers,
free of the silence of our mothers

Could have burnt down those oblivious
buildings, erased the blind
teachers and social workers
torn up the papers that purported
to explain, deleted the files
submitted for the attention of…

If you'd only had the time,
there would have been time,

to open the curtains
and find the world still there

MY STORY

The thing is this:
you have ruined my story,
disrupted the narrative,
the laws of causality.
Disorder – after some confusion,
rejection, cliff-hanging indecision,
leading to order: a marriage, a birth

Yet now I find myself at *The End*
amidst the debris of mistakes
Confusion, rejection.
No cliff-hangers then
perhaps just a hanging

My death by rope?
No, rather a slow ageing,
a gentle verging on the ridiculous
the unforgivable sin of having lost youth
and husband.

DIGNITY

I would have preferred a dead husband.
I could have risen to meet black
with the clenched jaw of decorum,
I would have made peace with
the lesson on transience,
obeyed the command of halted time
with clods of dark earth
thrown into the void.
I could have worn the widow's face
with entitlement, instead
of the maudlin misery
of abandonment.
The 'grown apart',
the 'different paths',
the pantomime pleasantries
made for parlour tragedies.
I have skidded around
the edge of grief,
and muddied my arse.
Soiled with the stain
of self-indulgence
in a world where
only death maintains
the final dignity.

UNDERWRITTEN

I've already accounted for
the anniversaries missed,
the ones past
and those still to come

I've underwritten
your liability
with my tears, and
my womanly ailments

I hearthed my fire,
dammed my flood,
clenched my jaw,
while you spoke
of property and crockery

Once I sacrificed a child
at the threshold of our home
you walked on it each day
oblivious, healthy,
while I felt every step.

DEAD WEIGHT

The dead weight of your love
has kept me treading water for so long,
near to drowning yet somehow just
keeping head above surface.

The dead weight of your silence
has left me choking on my own words
Mouthfuls of frustration
and biting irony

The weight of inertia
has dulled and flattened
and left me no footholds
on the smooth slope of descent

I'm sodden with the weight of old love
of words and gestures misunderstood
My weakened limbs strain to reach you,
while trying to save myself

Can the sun reach inside me now?
Wring my veins; smooth the nerves
and tendons. Splay my soaked skin
in thin blue layers under its heat?

Nothing else will do.

UNANSWERED

Our parting is like
an unanswered question
disturbing the very flow
of conscious time.

In the dark hours it visits
like a nervous animal
approaching, losing confidence,
retreating, then watching from a corner.

Daytime, it crouches
glancing up momentarily
with green eyes, intent on the hunt,
on the endless task of chasing its own tail.

I travel to other places only to know
they exist, to find a reality with a past
that is not ours. I seek the relief
of your absence and the balm of anonymity.

WRITING POEMS

I sit writing poems
while you busy yourself with life
I make wagers with myself
while your absence rings in my ears
If I could will you to hear me
I would not be here now
and the space around me
would be full

I sit writing poems
while you negotiate and discuss
you rule and are accountable
but I have opted out
of the business of life
and I sit writing poems
on your time and
on your account

I weigh up my words
on each end of the scales
that is me in the morning
and me at night
There is no judge presiding
nor jury in the box
You keep the silence
of the one who has left

And all these words
cannot settle the balance sheet
or pay the bills
I take the high ground
while you tread the land
tend the plants
and buy the food
that feeds the bellies

I have not been fair
with you. I have not
paid my way
in order to be forgiven
I must forgive
and render unto you
all that is rightly yours
for better or for worse

I have destroyed
too much that wasn't mine
– torn-up pictures
and deleted lines
that were not written by me –
You can take the sum
of who I am and
reckon the grand total

The kindness along
with the accusations
The hurt along
with the truth
I sit writing poems
for someone who has
no love for them
and the shortfall
remains our debt.

FUTURE, IMAGINED

I imagined an old age
the chiselling of your cheekbones
smudged. My golden hair
paled.

I remember a couple
sat impossibly far back
on a window ledge at
the National Portrait Gallery.

Their little legs, foreshortened,
made them look like dolls
holding hands with a childishness
not enough cherished, in the aging.

I imagined companionship,
an equalizing of prescriptions
so that I could read you road signs
while you read me menus.

I thought that love would last till death.
I thought that friends would not die young.
There's a riddle in there somewhere,
or perhaps a pun.

DIVORCE

I broke our contract
on the last hot day of the year

The improper sun seared
too bright on my cool anger

I'd mourned all through summer
through tendon and nerve

One leg buckled, swerved
the other, strong and striding

With these two syllables dividing
what was once the dream of two

Now just the turn of the screw
outgrown Church and Hollywood

Together we divide what should
not be parted by any hand

But you must know, as a man
that fortune favours the brave

And that my tears could not save
any other than my own self

Yet I have my grandma's hands
strong enough to claim my lands

And I shall live by the sea
with one who loves me

INHERITANCE

My grandma's hands
were her abiding feature
they saw her through
Hitler's bombs, my grandfather's
rages and decades of sleeping pills
on which she blamed
all her bad decisions.

Still smooth, though
peppered with liver spots
(I balked at 'grave marks')
they wove their own stories
from coloured wool and clacking needles
spent their days in service
baking, basting, bestowing.

My hands too, seek
creativity, strive to redress
the balance, to produce
more good than harm. And
I shall one day rise from my chair
like a teenager, only to learn
that time has over-taken me.

Shall I claim my matriarchal
legacy to age alone?
There are so many days
to fill, and such small imagination;
We can think of nothing
better than this: to divide
things, space, future.

It may be enough to say
that I loved and was loved
my grandma died never
having kissed with passion
I plead *not guilty* to that
only guilty of too much
gave tendon, muscle, limb.

This ache will endure, of course,
despite our skilful carelessness
despite the wilful sabotages
for only God knows how to
close that particular door
and neither of us is sure, he exists
There's always more, more, more.

NOT ANGER

You called it anger,
it was simply
the subterfuge of fear.

You cried 'hysteria!'
The voice of the womb
that mothered our child?

You called it paranoia,
but my heart is a lodestone,
compassing.

And my True North
is your Arctic. Exposed
to the elements
stripped of cover

An inhospitable place for
a creature of camouflage,
adapted to feign with the foliage,
the pampas of politesse.

Nature has no mercy
for our frail human shelters.
Beyond this point only
wide ocean and ice-flow

While your mind charters
the contours of precipice,
attempting to part land from water
emotion from logic

the great thaw is already begun
and falling is easier in surrender
than resistance.

TO YOU

Something you said today –
the possibility to knock on my door
if you were sure –
made me understand
that could never happen

whilst I must compete
with the cleanness of numbers
the sturdiness of marble
the glitter of competence.

My feminine conceit thinly
conceals sweat and blood,
sticky words remembered,
the odour of transgressions
still un-forgiven.

I bequeath you your lands,
your right to dominion
I skirt the borders of your manhood
like a cat seeking an open window.

To you the bread-
winning, the hard-
working. The respect.
To me, poetry.

STORY

I

It started with an averted gaze, your eyes skimmed across my face a little too quickly. Your gaze no longer met mine in complicity. I thought it no more than freak weather – the light dusting of sand from a distant desert.

II

Your eyes, a green reflection of mine, became lost in the detail of everyday, the comfort of sums and solutions. Losing their movement, their capacity to shift between perspectives. The linear trajectory of intent has no inkling of the space required for intimacy.

III

While you conjured an execution from the air, I lined up my stories like discarded dolls along the top of the wardrobe. And one by one you removed the stuffing of meaning, unaware that outside our theatre lay the grotesque, the uncomprehending world of cause and effect.

IV

I continued to play my creation myth without an audience. The tales I told of our love revolved on their axis like prayers sent up to the heavens. But prayers, like poetry, are intelligible only to those who comprehend the language of despair and hope.

V

Soon, my feet lost their ground, my muscles strained against gravity; so when I tumbled, it was with the inevitability of a felled tree. A question of need and commerce, you said, as you gathered me from the floor. No time to mourn the view, you departed.

VI

And as you left, every time you left, you went beyond the reach of the words we had shared; entered the world of transactions, where all that is given freely is without value. Our life viewed through the wrong end of a telescope: small, distant, insignificant.

VII

There are secrets buried in each of us: hard-boiled, felted by swell and undercurrent. I plucked mine from the heart of me, and like a crazed witness at the guillotine, picked it apart fibre by fibre. Intent on the task at hand, I never noticed the blood on the walls.

VIII

And blood is not your thing. You no longer slept in our bed – little knowing that the past walks through walls, along cables and into the words lodged in your ears at night. Its pays no heed to the light that wards off my nightmares, nor the skull's helmet of logic.

IX

I had feared my own dark dreams so long, I failed to notice the shadows move across your face. Or else I thought them a reflection. But mirrors can be deceptive, throwing back not just reality inverted, but a new world, unexpected. And true couples are

their own reflection, a coupling not only in the eyes. We walk the earth, our hands clasped. We stand together in photographs, projecting to the future, unaware that these images are no more. It makes no difference – the drawers no longer hold your possessions, but memory encompasses.

X

Why this greed to tell your story, this insatiable desire for the fulfilment of narrative? As in centuries past, I sit with household animals around the fire, waiting for story to banish time and absurdity. This scavenging hunger will leave no meat left on our bones.

XI

If we can accept the miracle of the world's beginnings, life created in one explosion, why can't we believe the metaphors written within our cells, the body's relentless urge to express not through words, but with the prophesy of pain. The language of organs, muscle and vein.

XII

If I save a place for trespasses forgiven, will that possibility be returned by you? The trading of hurt through generations has left a surplus upon our bodies, and the time of reckoning is at hand. And our weapon of choice, only tenderness.

THE LAST PAGE

You have looked for too long,
at your own reflection, in the eyes
of others. Spent too many hours,
in the shadow of your own achievements.

Beneath your robes of office,
lies something as small as a foetus, pulsing
with another heartbeat. A quiet waiting –
in suspension – to come into being.

I dare not call you from the amniotic fluid
of forgetting, I must not disturb
the delicate balance of survival, until
the time of blood and pain and living is here.

If I could write your body, as so many men
have written women; our heavy thighs, our breasts,
our necks, I'd conjure the rising hill of your shoulder,
the gentle slope of pectoral muscle.

As my tongue seeks the familiar indentations
and smooth surfaces of the teeth inside my mouth,
so my mind encompasses – strokes – the movements
of your body in space. Our space.

I would, I would, I would. Save. Carry.
Digest. But we can both recall my surrender
at the feet of your absence. The narrative
passes to you, to write your own past and therefore

your future. Naming is itself an act of rebellion
and a promise of healing. I pass you the pen,
the book and the scream. We can wait until the moment
of death, and even then – have hope.

BIOGRAPHICAL NOTE

S. D. CURTIS is a publisher, author and sometime translator from Croatian / Bosnian. She studied literature and public art at Roehampton University and has an MA in Education (Applied Linguistics). Her novels *So Like Fire* (1998) and *Leave to Remain* (2007) were originally self-published and have since been translated and published in Croatia. She has lived and worked for long periods in Rome, Ljubljana and Zagreb and presently does both in Camden, London.